Other books in this series:

Welsh Pottery

WELSH QUILTS

by

Jen Jones

A TOWY GUIDE

TOWY PUBLISHING

First Impression: 1997
Reprinted: 2003

Copyright © Jen Jones 1997

Published by
Towy Publishing, Cwmoernant House, Carmarthen, SA31 1EG

Printed by
Gwasg Dinefwr Press, Llandybie, Carmarthenshire.

ISBN 0 9525790 1 4

Front cover:
Central Star quilt made in Aberdare, by Sarah Lewis in 1875

Back cover:
Red paisley quilts.

Acknowledgements

THE CONCEPT OF A SERIES OF GUIDES covering various aspects of Welsh heritage is a splendid one, and I am so pleased Robert Pugh asked me to contribute towards it by writing about Welsh quilts.

I am most grateful to David Welch for his stellar editorial and proof-reading assistance. I thank Janet Bridge, Hazel Newman and Sherry Wilson for keeping people at bay, thus permitting me to concentrate on the task in hand. Special thanks to Sherry who masterminded the wordprocessor, never complaining when I asked for yet another draft.

I would also like to thank Pete Davies for his marvellous photography; all photographs not otherwise credited are by him. Thanks also to my husband Roger for his moral support and Kate for being patient.

Very special thanks to all the individuals I encountered over the years on farms and in towns who shared their knowledge with me, thus contributing so much to this book.

For Mal

Contents

Introduction

As I write, ten of my favourite, and most travelled quilts are in England, where they are being shown in a number of museums and galleries. If you live in the right part of the UK (or of America or Japan) you may have a chance to see them. Nothing, of course, is quite as good as having them under your direct gaze, but I hope this little book will evoke something of their beauty, charm and interest, and that the illustrations will serve as a reasonable substitute for a private viewing of my collection.

This is not likely to impress anyone as a highly erudite tome. To be honest, I have not spent too much time in the libraries. You are more likely to find me jolting my car down a rugged farm track, or ferreting in a dusty attic, in some hidden corner of the Welsh hills, ever hopeful of bringing the ultimate wholecloth back into the light. For the past 25 years, I have bought quilts to collect, sold them (often with reluctance), cleaned, repaired and restored them. So, it is the quilts themselves and information gleaned from their former owners that constitute my real source material. My private collection now numbers over one hundred, but hundreds more have passed through my hands. Each of them has added something to my knowledge of this vanished craft, and almost always heightened my admiration for an artistry that has been too little recognised and often undervalued. Those quilts that have survived (sadly, many have not) come into our own times as living emissaries of another age, when there was a different way of doing things. They evoke the dexterity, imagination and creativeness of people who could produce such wonderful artefacts from such humble and limited resources.

I shall concentrate on a hundred year period (roughly 1840–1940), including the most prolific period (1880–1935) during which time the bulk of Welsh quilting was produced. My aim is to touch on all the various types of quilts, the people who made them, regional variations and the reasons for the ultimate decline in production. I feel that no study of Welsh quilts can totally exclude mention of the Welsh woollen blanket, and consequently I will add a little about this marvellous allied commodity which has only recently begun to be appreciated as a craft of infinite skill, variety and beauty.

History

ALTHOUGH QUILTING IN WALES CAN BE traced to the 17th and 18th centuries and even earlier, examples from that period are primarily articles of clothing, particularly of the military kind. Quilted undergarments worn beneath armour afforded warmth and protection. Domestically, caps and underslips shielded the wearer from the cold. Quilted bedcovers were to be found but the majority were simply utilitarian. Usually the outer layers were rough heavy worsted, or scraps of woollen fabric encasing an old blanket or two. The object was warmth, not beauty. Towards the end of the 18th century and into the 19th some decorative, ornamental quilts appeared but they were the province of the wealthy, and output was comparatively small, consisting mainly of patchwork in early chintzes with exceptionally fine stitchwork and elaborate quilting patterns or ingenuous endeavours by the younger girls of the household. The earliest dated quilt in my own collection is 1807 initialled AM aged 15! The maker was one of the daughters of a well-to-do Pembrokeshire family. Between 1800 and 1850 many one-of-a-kind quilts were made, again, more often than not, by girls from affluent homes as part of those sewing skills that young ladies preparing for marriage were expected to acquire. Among these were some fine silk, velvet and ribbon patchworks. Few of these have survived intact as the shellac used to stiffen silks and taffeta eventually rotted these materials leaving the quilts in tatters. Not until the second half of the 19th century could quilting be classified as a craft industry in Wales. Fabrics were too dear to be easily afforded by the poorer classes who relied on homespun woollen blankets, either individually or roughly quilted together, for their bedding. Less expensive roller-printed fabrics became widely available about 1840, and with the introduction of

Early utilitarian quilted bedcover.

11

these, quilt production soared. The mid 19th century also witnessed a resurgence in the output of Welsh flannel, and some of the most exciting of all the Welsh quilts ever made resulted from the abundance of this wonderful material in bold blues, reds, blacks and, to a lesser extent, greens. The geometric flannel patchworks which evolved are, understandably, frequently compared to the Amish quilts in the United States. When the use of colour, the stripes or bars, the prominent shapes and even, to a certain extent, the quilting patterns of the quilts from the two countries are compared, the similarities are striking. I am in no doubt that the influx of the Welsh and their culture into parts of the United States, particularly Pennsylvania, had an influence on Amish quilt designs across the Atlantic. The Amish are still commercially producing their quilts whereas, unhappily, 70 to 80 years have elapsed since the same could be said for the Welsh. What is undeniable, is the dramatic character inherent in both.

Satin-cotton in plain colours as well as patterned or floral became very popular, and wholecloth quilts made from these dominated the scene between 1880–1940.

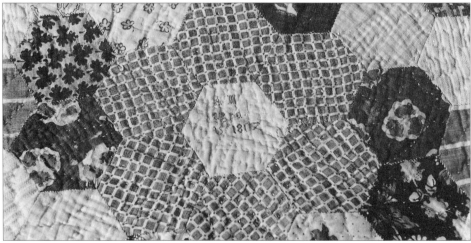

Two early examples of signed and dated quilts made by young ladies from fine households, both Pembrokeshire.

Between 1880 and the demise of quilting as a Welsh cottage industry (c.1940) the most popular quilts were those made from solid coloured, floral and patterned satin-cotton. This material was the dominant quiltmaking fabric for over half a century.

The cosy notion of the sewing bee, where the ladies of the community get together to quilt and gossip, was not a Welsh concept. Although sometimes quilts were made in the home by the women of the household or in groups such as the Women's Institute, the vast majority were sewn by professionals. Quiltmaking was a paid occupation, not a hobby. It was one of the few available means by which a Welsh woman could earn a living. It offered a livelihood to many a miner's widow (pensions and compensation were unheard of at the turn of the century) left to support four or five small children as well as herself. She could choose between domestic work, selling herself, or the needle. Quilting was a means by which she could remain at home and still eke out a respectable livelihood. Spinsters of slender means also frequently turned to sewing as a means of support. A splendid example of this was a single lady, Miss Nanci Lewis, living on the outskirts of Llandeilo. She devoted approximately 12 hours out of every 24 to sewing and quilting. She suffered from excruciatingly severe migraines but would not allow them to deter her from her task. She merely wound a wet handkerchief around her head and persevered. Her quilts were of the finest, and greatly in demand. Every household aspired to one of her 'specials', and her dowry quilts were a prerequisite for every bride-to-be's bottom drawer. On she toiled, year after year, until suddenly at age 60 she met a local widower with whom she fell in love and promptly married, never to pick up her needle again, or to endure another migraine – we sincerely hope! It was the seamstresses in the towns and villages who quilted to order for the housewives living around them. Annually, if she could afford it, the mistress of the house would buy fabric for a new quilt from her local shop or from a travelling salesman from England. She would take it to the village quilter, along with her choice of wadding, and her winter bedding would be replenished. Perhaps she would dispose of one of her old quilts, somewhat the worse for wear, or extra fabric could be purchased, and that too would be sent for recovering. Almost every household kept aside at least one 'special' quilt for important occasions, such as a visit from a faraway relative, or more prosaically, the local GP. I bought a very fine quilt in Capel Dewi known as the 'invalid quilt', as it only emerged during illness and convalescence. Quilters sewed alone or with an apprentice, commonly the daughter of a local family willing to pay up to £2 for her to train under a professional. This meant staying with her teacher for a year, after which time she would be quite proficient in a trade that was regarded as appropriate for a girl with no great expectations. Some quilters were itinerants journeying from farm to farm, usually accompanied by their apprentice. They would board at a farm for approximately a fortnight or until completion of the quilt, at which point they would travel on to the next farmhouse, roughly one pound the richer. One awesome quilter in West Wales, Mary Jones (who died around 1900) was ambidextrous and could produce, when pushed, two quilts in a week – a staggering feat which must remain the all-time record for speed.

The quilter was not expected to provide anything but her expertise: the fabric and filling were always supplied by the farmers wife. Although some itinerants only felt comfortable working with their own frames, most were happy not to be burdened on their travels, and a frame was standard farm equipment waiting to be dusted off for the quilter's annual visit. Many farmsteads were remote, and visitors infrequent, so to a considerable extent it was a social event mutually anticipated by both quilter and farmer's wife. Sometimes the sojourn would be extended to carry out repairs, recover an old quilt or possibly produce a new dress or two.

Sadly as the 20th century got under way, Welsh quilting was on the wane. The financial returns, given the time involved, became less acceptable, and quilters found it harder to survive on what they earned. Following the 1914–1918 war, there was a further noticeable decline. Mass produced coverlets such as the 'Comfy', white counter-panes (including the marcellas), tapestry bedspreads and eiderdowns consumed a large portion of the market. Another factor contributing to the decline of the hand-sewn quilt was the exodus of young women from towns and villages to work for the war effort. They no longer had the time or the inclination to master the techniques, or they were not willing to train for an occupation so time-consuming and exacting yet so unremunerative.

Between the wars, there was a resurgence of quilting which owed itself, to some extent, to the efforts of the amateur Women's Institute quilters but, to a greater extent, to a programme established by the Rural Industries Bureau in 1928. The purpose of this scheme was to stimulate craft industries in parts of Wales where borderline poverty prevailed as, the depression took its toll. The more expert rural quilters, par-ticularly those in the valleys, were encouraged to perfect their techniques and refine their workmanship. They were financially assisted in obtaining the fabrics and filling but the Bureau didn't buy the finished products; it placed them with commercial galleries which found outlets in Cardiff and London for them. The quilts produced

Quilt made to compete in the Neath Eisteddfod 1934.

Back and front of finely stitched pillow shams made during the Rural Industries Bureau period.

around this period were some of the finest ever to be made in Wales, as standards had to be of the highest. These quilts and pillow shams were to adorn the beds of the best hotels; Claridges, The Dorchester, Grosvenor House. Many were destined for the aristocracy and some for the Royals themselves. How far this resurgence would have progressed one can only speculate. I feel the Welsh quilt might well still exist today as a commercial entity if the Second World War had not intervened. Unfortunately, with the outbreak of hostilities, the Rural Industries project was abandoned and everything it had engendered ground to a halt. Since the War, there have been attempts to bring about a revival. Notably, in 1950, the newly founded Welsh Folk Museum at St Fagan's ran a conference which resulted in a competition and exhibition the following year, but this and other enterprises met with great interest but only limited success. Post-war, a few women did continue to quilt professionally and to teach their subject. There was, and there still is, the indomitable Katy Lewis, the doyenne of Welsh quilters; and there was Mrs Thomas who lived at the foot of the Black Hills near Llangadog, in West Wales, making dowry quilts until shortly before her death in 1970. These and a few others soldiered on but they were exceptional, and as only a handful made a living from quilting it could no longer be considered an economically sustainable craft industry.

The current 'revival', spearheaded by the enthusiastic American traditionalists and by the Quilters Guild, has produced some fine quilts but the majority are patchwork, not typical Welsh wholecloth, and the numbers are minuscule compared to the thousands upon thousands produced in the heyday of this most exciting and colourful of Welsh crafts. The traditional Welsh quilt is now a finite commodity. It is an integral part of the Welsh heritage which until recently was seldom acknowledged as such. Far from showing them proper respect, housewives looked upon their quilts as 'old beddin' and discarded them indiscriminately. Some were recycled as tractor covers, draft excluders, lagging for hot water tanks or protection for the vegetable garden. These unique creations were on the brink of extinction. It was left to museums, quilters from other countries and enthusiasts of fine hand-crafts to appreciate and safeguard them. Twenty-five years ago they could be found at auction houses amidst bundles of household linen, auctioneers begging for a 'pound the lot'. Happily, today this is no longer the case, and it is not only those from abroad who esteem the Welsh quilt. Slowly but surely, the Welsh themselves are beginning to value this important part of their culture. The current generation saw their mothers and grandmothers cover sick cows or frost endangered potato beds with them, or worse still, throw their old quilts on the bonfire. Luckily, attitudes have changed. The young women of today are eager to obtain a Welsh quilt of their own, thus acquiring a significant piece of Welsh history to treasure and preserve.

Making a Quilt

Before discussing the different types of Welsh quilts, it is helpful to say a little about two aspects of their composition that help distinguish them from all others and contributes greatly to their overall effect: what they were filled with and the stitching patterns to be found within their borders.

The most common batting materials were blankets and lambswool. The former was used a great deal as it was a way of recycling a thinning or damaged blanket and at the same time, of gaining extra warmth. The more threadbare the blanket the more successful as padding. If it was too thick and rigid the quilting would, naturally, be less well-defined: lambswool was ideal as the inner layer. It was supple, soft and malleable, enhancing the stitchwork considerably. This assumed of course, that it had been prepared correctly. About two pounds of wool was needed to line a quilt adequately. It was usually collected from the hedgerows, as this cost nothing, and it had to be washed in soapy water and dried thoroughly on a bright and breezy day (some natural oil, thought to deter moths, was left in on purpose.) before being

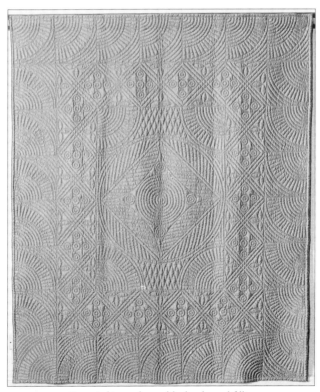

Fine stitching enhanced by lambswool filling.

Another star quilt by Sara Lewis of Aberdare, with startling green and purple.

Central pinwheel, c.1850, Cardiganshire, one of very few 'double' patchworks.

Large pinwheel in navy and red with fine stitchwork, Cardiganshire, c.1875.

Carding brushes, wool and woolsack pegs.

carded with wire brushes . To be sure, the wool was not always prepared with as much care as it deserved. I have encountered quilts where the wool mingled with thistles and twigs and, horrors, pellets of sheep dung. The only answer to the last was to soak the quilt for over a week to encourage the impurities to disperse.

Cotton wadding was purchased as filling by a few professional quiltmakers but used far less in Wales than in other parts of the world. The great advantage of cotton is that it simplifies laundering as the dangers of bunching and shrinkage are considerably reduced. In Wales lambswool was readily available, inexpensive and perfect for the task in hand. However, a lambswool quilt must always be washed by hand in cold or lukewarm water and never, never placed in a drier.

Utilitarian quilts have been known to encase old shirts, stockings and even feathers with no regard as to whether or not any of these were colourfast. I bought a quilt once that had never been laundered. It was in a cotton print which I felt sure was colourfast. When I washed it an enormous blue patch appeared in the middle which refused to disappear as it dried. A piece of indigo dyed fabric was the villian having been placed with an assortment of cloth remnants as part of the wadding. Alas, the quilt was unredeemable. The ultimate thrifty quilt was an old one recovered – sometimes two, three or even four times. These were ungainly, unsightly and probably extremely unsanitary due to the impossibility of washing them thoroughly, but, my goodness, they were warm!

Quilting patterns did vary from region to region in Wales but it is difficult to confuse a typical wholecloth Welsh quilt with a North Country English (Durham) quilt or a European or American one. The individual patterns and combinations of designs are distinctive, and although they range from the extremely simple to the immensely complex, they have features in common that are readily recognisable. The designs in Welsh quilting tend to be more geometric in character than the more fluid and flowery motifs of the North Country and Wessex quilts. Generally, an American quilt will tell a story in patchwork or appliqué, whereas its Welsh equivalent will paint a portrait through stitchwork. A typical Welsh quilt has a large circular medallion in the centre, often surrounded by smaller motifs, which are enlarged and repeated as the quilting works outwards towards a border, which can introduce new designs of its own or reflect those in the centre . The motifs encountered most often are leaves, flowers, acorns and feathers (all reflecting nature); triangles (mainly used as in-fill), half-fans, fans, hearts, Prince of Wales feathers and the time-honoured snail or spiral which circles about, never closing, and was believed by many to represent a long life, and even eternity. Two other small motifs commonly found are tulips and the Welsh pear, known across the border as paisley seed pod. A fine repre-

Typical Welsh quilting patterns surrounding large central medallion.

Red and navy small pinwheel flannel quilt with pinwheel corners,
Cross Inn, Cardiganshire, 1890.

Bold squares and rectangles, c.1880, Synod Inn.

Diagonal Bow Tie flannel, Mydroilyn, c.1890.

Large central Bow Tie with splendid geometric surround, Llandeilo, c.1880.

Various items used to trace patterns on Welsh quilts (plate, cup, etc.).
(Photograph: Hazel Newman).

Cardboard and paper templates.
(Photograph: Hazel Newman).

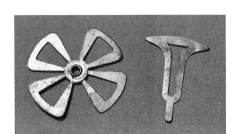

Metal template.

sentative Welsh quilt will incorporate as many as ten different motifs. Patterns were passed on by teacher to pupil and from family to family, finally to be defined and labelled as indigenous toward the end of the quilting era in the 1930s. Motifs were traced onto the fabric prior to quilting, most often with tailor's chalk. Glasses, cups and plates were among the objects employed for this, as were pieces of cardboard cut out to the required shape, and occasionally, custom-made metal templates. Rulers were used for edges, corners and straight line work within the quilt. Some more expert quilters chalked their designs freehand, whilst a very few of great expertise, proceeded without any tracing of any kind. What is most refreshing about Welsh quilts is that they do not always adhere to the rules as practised by the quilters of today. A fine quilter executing her craft could break the rules, even supposing she was aware that there were rules, and get away with it. In fact, by breaking them, she often produced a work of art without intending to. Although the remuneration was very small, sewing was her job, and she had to get on with it as there was always the next quilt, and the next, waiting to be made. The work achieved was ingenuously refreshing, if not always strictly precise. What good is it to follow the old so-many-stitches-to-the-inch dictum if the end result is tortured, self-conscious and lacks spontaneity and artlessness? A modern quilter often tries too hard and probably has an open-ended completion date. There is a lot to be said for the discipline of necessity. Today, quilting is looked upon as a craft that is an art form. The main body of Welsh quilting was far more prosaic. Quality varied tremendously, depending upon the imagination and skill of the quilter and the materials to hand, but the amazing diversity amongst them is indisputable.

Method

V ERY NEARLY WITHOUT EXCEPTION, quilts in Wales were made on a frame. This consisted of four pieces of wood: two long bars with webbing nailed on one side for attaching the quilt and two smaller cross pieces which slotted into apertures on the bars. Each of these pieces had a number of holes into which pegs were placed to hold the bars firm. Relatively few of these ungainly implements remain. Most were stored in outbuildings where they were prime targets for woodworm. Not considered worth treating and preserving, the majority have been chopped up for firewood.

Frame inscribed "Evans Bwlch, Bangor 1860".

Assembled frame.

Frame with half-made quilt.

Central Star 1870, Llanrhystud (found between the mattress and springs).

*Interesting geometric, cotton lining flannel
and furnishing fabric, c.1925.*

Mid 19th century grey black and red flannel patchwork, Pembrokeshire.

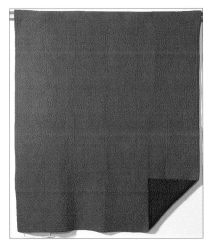

Green and red flannel wholecloth,
Cardiganshire, c.1890.

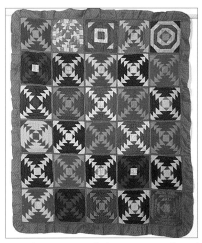

Thirty squares of 'Flying Geese' in flannel
and wool, Aberystwyth, 1905.

Assortment of wooden pegs used on frames.

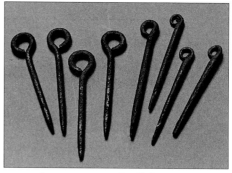

Less common metal quilt frame pegs.

A quilt by definition consists of two pieces of fabric placed either side of a layer of wadding and then stitched together. The best Welsh quilts, in my opinion, surpass all others in the variety and intensity of the stitching patterns used to join these three layers. A wholecloth Welsh quilt with intricate stitching patterns is a marvellous thing but when really subtle imaginative patchwork meets intricate quilting, especially among the Pembrokeshire quilts, the result is superlative.

Solid and floral satin cotton.

Details from beautifully quilted satin cotton quilt.

Types of Quilts

THE WOOLLEN QUILT

AS WE'VE ALREADY SEEN, the majority of the very early woollen Welsh quilts were purely utilitarian and extremely crude. Some we now consider to have a certain ethnic charm but for the most part they were inelegant with little artistic merit.

From the latter half of the 19th century into the 20th, a wide assortment of woollen quilts was produced, ranging from the basic to the supreme. Tailors' sample quilts appeared in large numbers. These consisted of small squares or rectangles of flannel, serge and tweed, taken principally from sample books, sewn together and backed with lengths of woollen cloth. Very often these were straight patchwork with very little lining or stitchwork. The majority are in browns, blacks and greys; not especially colourful, but an excellent catalogue of the woollen fabrics available at that time. Frequently, two contrasting plain woollen colours were combined. When lined with blankets, the cover produced would be extremely heavy with minimal quilting. When filled with fleece and stitched elaborately with heart, leaf, flower and diamond motifs, the resulting quilt could be every bit as elegant as some of its satin-cotton contemporaries. My favourite combination of solid flannels is the red and green which, of course, are the national colours of Wales .

Log cabin, church house steps, flying geese and even more intricate woollen patchworks were made in Wales but it is the large daring geometrics that are most stunning to behold. Depending on the ability of the maker and the filling used (lambswool accentuating the stitchwork best), quilting on these covers can be very simple or exceptionally complex. It is, however, the combination and composition of the bold-coloured flannel pieces that makes these the works of art they undoubtedly are. They usually feature a sizeable central motif such as star, bow-tie, pinwheel or square with simple blocks of colour working towards corners which frame the whole. Occasionally, appliqué hearts were used for highlighting the central motif, and possibly the corners, but for the most part it is the stark architectural quality that makes these quilts so thrilling. There are relatively few survivors in any of the woollen categories, as so many were destroyed either by rodents, the ever prevalent moth, strenuous washing or unwitting owners who failed to recognise their importance. One of the favourites in my collection was found between the box-spring and mattress in a house in Llanrhystud. It had been relegated to this lowly position by two dear, well-meaning old ladies who thought it bulky and unsightly. They were greatly surprised to be offered more for it than for the flowery satin-cottons they displayed with such pride!

The best Welsh flannel patchworks are enormously exciting. They are as spectacular

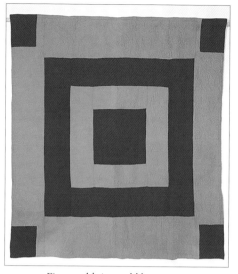

Flying Geese in flannel, Aberaeron, 1910.

Fine wool beige and blue squares,
Meidrim, Carmarthenshire, c.1900.

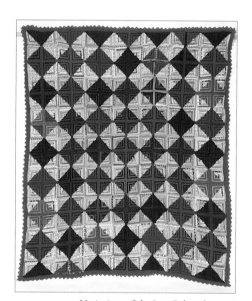

Variations of the Log Cabin design, Lampeter. Left: c.1880; right: Horeb 1888.

Two paisley shawl quilts.

Printed shawl quilted with solid colour back.

Woven shawl bordered with red paisley fabric.

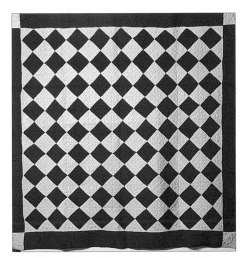

Dramatic purple and cream fine woollen patchwork, made near Aberystwyth, c.1875.

Tailors Sample quilt, Lampeter, Velufy, 1895.

as any quilts to be found anywhere, and they represent to me the craft's greatest contribution to the world of quilting. A personal bias perhaps, but one that is now acknowledged by a widening circle of collectors and enthusiasts.

COTTON

The vast majority of Welsh quilts (1880–1940) were made from cotton, and satin-cotton. The latter was a fine soft cotton fabric that only lost its sheen after years of use and repeated washings. It then appeared as a flat cotton which was still perfectly acceptable if not quite as decorative. Quilters claim this to be the most marvellous material to sew. For many years it has been unavailable. A facsimile has recently been imported from Egypt, but it is difficult to find and very expensive. Probably the best example of Welsh stitching patterns can be found on plain coloured satin-cotton quilts made during the height of the Rural Industries Bureau period – those made for sale to a fastidious, elite, urban market.

Satin-cotton was available in solid colours, prints and florals. Very often the quilt top would be floral, the back a solid colour. Some claim that the floral side was for everyday use as it did not show the odd grubbiness or spill. It would be reversed to the plain side for visitors or special occasions. Among the finer examples, both sides were beautiful, and today people often choose to display the 'back', as the portrait in stitching stands out so intensely when not overpowered by busy patterns.

Another popular combination was a floral or print using one set of colours on one side, and the same print in other colours on the reverse. Two totally different prints or florals were also frequently used as back and front – not always harmoniously.

Contrasting solids were another favourite. Unfortunately there were several popular combinations that today we find too garish to live with. A particularly virulent pink commingling with blue was enormously fashionable in the twenties and thirties, as was a lurid avocado and gold duo. No matter how splendid the quilting, I would not be able to live with either. I love the all-whites, the creams, pastel pinks and blues and the pale yellows.

Regrettably, the plain colours, particularly the deeper tones such as reds, blues and

Queen Victoria's Golden Jubilee. Slightly anomalous in that it is a Welsh quilt featuring the English and Scottish emblems, and not the Welsh.

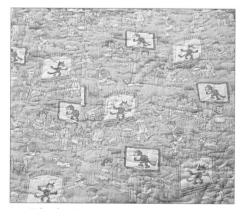

Felix the Cat on screen surrounded by young admirers.

greens, faded badly if exposed to light. Many solid tone quilts have been spoiled through ignorance. Once yearly, the quilts not in current use would be brought out of their linen presses for the summer airing, only to be refolded and stored in precisely the same manner as before. The exposed crease eventually faded, and when opened, the quilt would be marred by a central discolouration that cannot be corrected. The lesson to be learned is never to store a quilt folded the same way for too long. Take it out, air it, and refold it the opposite way. Never store a quilt in an airtight bag or near a hot water tank that might leak. Keep it away from direct sunlight, and don't forget most forms of moth protection last for a limited period. Over the years I have encountered many, many quilts that had been gorgeous in their day, inadvertently ruined by well-meaning owners ignorant of the vulnerability and fragility of textiles. For some strange reason, because they do not break, people assume quilts are indestructible.

RED PAISLEY

Red paisley was exceedingly popular for use in quiltmaking, especially during the late 19th and early 20th century, and the diversity of prints is glorious. As with busy florals, the stitching in these is substantially lost due to the complexity of the fabric design. However, they are vibrantly ornate and make wonderful decorative accessories avidly sought after by interior designers. Paisley-patterned fabrics were manufactured in other colours as well – black, green, usually the deeper tones, until the emergence of the pinks and pale blues of the 30s and 40s. A subtler version is the paisley-shawl quilt. Paisley shawls, either printed or woven, were occasionally used as tops, with plain reverse, or sometimes two printed shawls, or a woven and a printed, would be combined . Today, the shawls themselves are so costly that sacrificing one for quilting would be unusual, but 80 to 100 years ago, they were an everyday item, and, in combination with fleece lining, afforded a bedcover both aesthetically pleasing and extremely warm.

RED AND WHITE

A quantity of red and white quilts, almost invariably patchwork or strippy, were made in Wales, between 1850 and the First World War. I have been told by several old ladies that they were the preferred wedding quilt. Hearts do feature in many of them but, then again, heart motifs also appear in the florals and solids produced for general household use. One enlightened Welsh lady, a nurse married to a doctor, was prepared to give, rather than sell, to me the magnificent red and white she had inherited, so superstitious was she about its symbolising blood, gore and inevitable catastrophe. As with the bold flannels, Welsh red and whites have much in common with their American counterparts. Sometimes it is assumed they have actually been sent across the Atlantic, presents from emigrant relatives. Close perusal of the stitching patterns belies this.

'STRIPPY'

A typical Welsh 'strippy' quilt features two contrasting fabrics, joined in strips,

Two charming, naive Welsh patchworks featuring appliqué hearts in the centres, both, Pembrokeshire, latter quarter of the 19th century.

Quilted underskirt approximately 100 years old. Rescued from a costume box belonging to an amateur dramatic group.

A wedding quilt in satin cotton with elaborate stitching featuring hearts.
Carmarthenshire, c.1910.

Satin cotton wedding quilt made in 1920 in Newcastle Emlyn.
The time hearts are not featured.

approximately 6' to 8' in width, running the entire length of the quilt. I have yet to encounter a Welsh quilt with narrow stripes or ones framed within a border, both characteristic of the 'bar' quilt, its early American counterpart. Unlike its North Country English equivalent, where quilting patterns frequently are contained within the stripes, the quilting in a Welsh strippy works across the entire piece. Bold-coloured flannel in two colours (most often navy or black and red), cotton prints and florals in contrasting light and dark fabrics, red and white, or other complimentary solid coloured cottons were the most common choices for the Welsh 'strippy'.

COTTON PATCHWORKS

Professionally produced in fewer numbers, were the cotton patchworks. At their best, these descendants of the comparatively rare chintz patchworks combine fine colour combination and skilful quilting patterns. These could feature a central star surrounded by blocks, or project a kaleidoscopic effect with tiny pieces in the middle that grew as the quilt progressed outwards. Sometimes, remnants were utilised in these quilts (particularly in the crazy quilts), sometimes fabric samples, comparable to the woollen tailors quilt, but very often lengths of various complimentary textiles would be bought specifically, as was the case with the wholecloth florals and solids. The majority of scrap and random cotton patchworks were home-made, amateurish efforts, interesting only to the maker or for the variety of fabrics involved. Small mention should also be made of the 'poor man's' patchwork, which was made from patchwork printed material. Barring close scrutiny you believe the piece to be patchwork, and if backed in a solid colour and well quilted, the effect is splendid.

The reverse of an early 1840 chintz patchwork.
An intricately quilted potted plant forms the centre.

APPLIQUÉ

Although appliqué was not employed often in Welsh quilting, particularly not as an overall design, there were many notable exceptions. A certain Catherine James of Troed y Rhiw, between Brechfa and Llandovery, was renowned for her appliqué, and produced some beautiful examples, distinguished by their bold yet naive imagery, in two primary colours emblazoned on a white background. These could hold their own with most of their early American counterparts.

COT/CRIB QUILTS

Crib quilts were often made to order by the village quilter when a new baby was due, and would generally be used, in turn, by each new addition to the family. Condition of surviving crib quilts can be taken as a good indication of the number of children in a particular family! Patchwork was a favourite, (perhaps because staining was better disguised), but double-sided wholecloths were also popular. These almost always incorporated heart motifs among their designs. The majority of baby quilts average two feet by one-and-a-half, whereas the larger, rarer cot variety are approximately five by three feet. There is tremendous variety in the colours and designs of these miniature versions of the Welsh quilt, and they have, rightly, come into their own as collector items and wall hangings.

Patchwork crib quilt proudly displayed by Theadora Dacia Thomas, born 1901, of Lampeter Velfrey. It was made for her brother, born 1905.

Cot quilt with fine stitching and scalloped edges, made 1920 in Pontypridd.

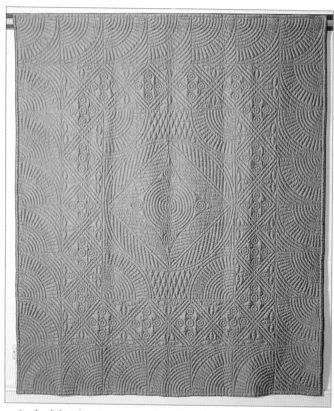

A splendid pink satin cotton quilt made in Cwrtnywedd, Cardiganshire, in 1933. The central medallion is surrounded by various patterns but fans predominate.

Detail of a Carmarthenshire quilt with elaborate stitching, featuring a large cross motif in the centre.

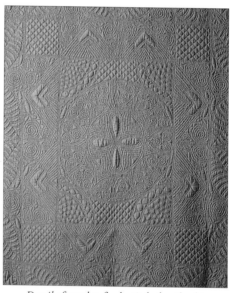

Detail of another finely stitched quilt, this time from West Glamorgan. It features pinwheel.

*Exuberant, bright, opaque appliqué quilt by
Catherine James of Troed y Rhiw 1895.*

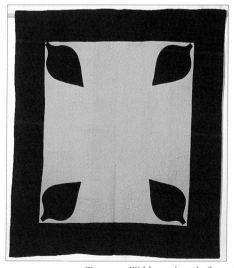 

Two zany Welsh patchworks from the valleys. Both 20th century, c.1920.

Joining and Finishing

Having discussed outer fabric, inner layer and motifs, some mention should be made of methods used to join lengths of fabric prior to quilting, the hemming of quilts, and the variety of edging styles.

Fabric varied in width but unless it was for a child's bed or baby's cot, more than one width of fabric was required for a full-sized quilt. Most commonly two, but quite often three lengths of fabric were joined for both the quilt top and back. Almost invariably, after 1890, the joins were machined, even when the entire quilt and the hemming was done by hand. Thrifty to a fault, even the professional, intent on avoiding waste, often refused to cut the fabrics in order to match up flowers or patterns. Nine times out of ten, this is insignificant, but it can be disconcerting, and in some cases I have known it to be so jarring as to ruin an otherwise beautiful quilt. The same applied to the plain coloured fabrics. Not infrequently, selvage edges can be seen on the joins; letters and numbers stamped upon them. By losing half-an-inch, this could have been avoided; but waste not, want not was the adage of the day, and it is a further illustration of the utilitarian, functional aspect of this craft industry. Conventionally, all four sides of a Welsh quilt are turned in at completion, and hand hemmed in a straight line. At times, however, a more ambitious quilter would choose

Pinked and perforated red flannel edging to a log cabin quilt.

Quilt with splendid pointed edges.
(Photograph: David Welch).

Double-sided flounce.
(Photograph: David Welch).

to scallop two sides of her quilt, and occasionally all four. The effect is fetching and warranted the extra effort in the hands of an expert. Occasionally, patchworks were backed in flannel which was pinked and perforated along the sides, and, once in a while, the maker would be totally innovative and edge her quilt with a zigzag or series of points. During the twenties and thirties, many of the satin-cotton quilts began to appear with a flounce or ruffle that framed the entire piece. Generally, this was of double thickness, each side matching the fabric of the corresponding side of the quilt. Whereas North Country English quilts were frequently as large as ten foot by eight foot, the unflounced Welsh equivalent measured on average only seven foot by six foot. A ruffle was considered decorative and could increase the length and width by up to ten inches each way to accommodate the larger beds that were appearing.

Examples of the variety of red and white quilts produced in Wales:

Red and white strippy with extraordinary stitchwork that won the price for the best quilt in Llanelli in 1901.

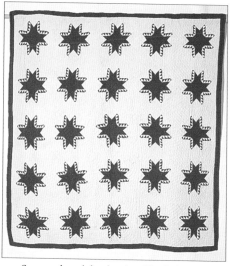

Star patchwork bordered and backed in red, and then quilted.

Unusual printed rectangle, featuring a border of artichokes, framed in red and quilted.

Red appliqué on white as hanging, with red and white patchwork on bed. Early cream and red blanket covers the chair and natural cream blankets hang at the windows.

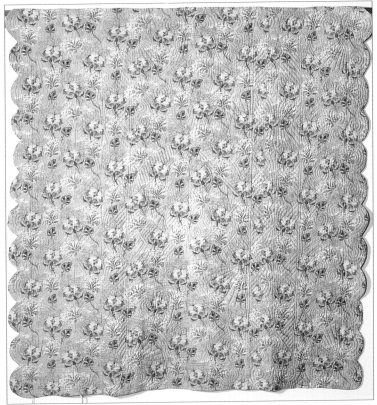

Art Nouveau floral with scalloped edges, Pontypridd, Glamorgan.

Two early Welsh cotton patchworks.
Left: Merthyr Tidfyl, c.1840. Right: Newcastle Emlyn, c.1850.

Provenance

EXACTLY WHERE A QUILT CAME FROM or who made it is a very grey area when looking at the vast majority of Welsh quilts. Yes, certain quilting patterns were associated more with one area than another, but seldom did an individual sign a quilt unless it was made by a family member as a future heirloom. The vast majority of quilts, made by the village and itinerant quilters, were acquired as bedding in much the same way that we might, today, go to a department store and buy a duvet. Seldom did it occur to either the maker or the purchaser to record a quilt's provenance. Often in my travels I have been told that, say, Mary Evans, made the quilt for the present owner's grandmother, or Siân Griffiths made it for great-aunt Sioned, but documentation is inclined to be sketchy, if it exists at all.

Certain quilters were renowned in particular areas and their work easily recognisable, but many times the work of lesser disciples was erroneously attributed to these women. Today very few quilts are not at least initialled, and the better known quilters who work on commissions always make sure posterity will credit them for their creations. It was not false modesty that prevented the quilters of the craft industry period from signing their work. Conceiving what they did as a utilitarian service, it would not have occurred to them to claim credit for their accomplishments.

A signed and dated quilt made by a Welsh woman who
emigrated to Canada and sent it back to a relation in Llanelli.

Buying a Welsh Quilt

I THINK THE MOST IMPORTANT CRITERION when buying a quilt is whether you like it or not. Nowadays people buy quilts mainly as decorative items. Occasionally they are to be slept under but for the most part they are to be used as bedcovers, throws or wall-hangings. More often than not, when quilts are to be bedspreads, they have to work in with a previously established decor. In an ideal world, first one should fall in love with a quilt, then proceed to decorate the room around it. I have never seen a room with quilts in it that wasn't warmed and enhanced by them. The marvellous variety of colours in the prints and florals can unleash all kinds of creative impulses and provide enormous enjoyment. If expensive patterned curtains and carpet are already in place, and finances prohibit starting from scratch, a solid coloured quilt might well be the answer. Choose one with good stitching patterns, in a shade you like, that blends in with everything else, and the effect will be both pleasing and restful. A complementary smaller quilt can be folded across the bottom of the bed, or tossed casually across the back of an armchair, to considerable effect. Strangely enough patchworks can work exceptionally well even if there are other busy patterns in the room. I think of them in much the same terms as oriental rugs which seem to blend so well with the other colours and designs surrounding them. In my own bedroom I have a quilt on the bed, one as an arras at the head of the bed, another on a side wall, and a smaller cot quilt high on the wall above the built in cupboards. A blanket covers a chair in the corner, which is adorned with quilted cushions. By using a neutral carpet and a pair of natural wool blankets as curtains I can, and do, have great fun transforming the entire room at least twice a year by exchanging all the quilts. For summer I might have red and white as a theme, autumn all red paisley, and in the winter I love to use the warm, dramatic flannels. The possibilities are endless.

Red and white bedroom.

Brilliant chintz patchwork, Pembrokeshire, c.1840. The magnificent quilting is somewhat overpowered by the wonderful prints, but, can be seen clearly on the reverse.

Detail of mauve and white Pembrokeshire patchwork, featuring a pot for its centre.

1807, Pembrokeshire, patchwork made by a girl of 15.

Cotton patchwork made in Cilcennin, Cardiganshire, c.1850.

Chintz patchwork, with large central panel, Swansea, c.1840.

When buying a quilt, condition is important if you are spending a fair amount of money. Look at the fabric closely, and, if it is thin or broken, then you know it will not sustain much wear and tear. If it is a patchwork, you might find that one particular material in it has deteriorated (often when early natural dyes have been used – particularly browns). If you are clever with a needle, and have access to compatible early fabrics, it would still be worth purchasing, if it really appeals to you and is not vastly expensive. Slightly damaged quilts still make very effective wall hangings, and they can also be gathered back as decorative curtaining or room dividers. They do wonders where there is an echo problem. Remember that a patchwork can be restored relatively easily, whereas a wholecloth quilt cannot. If a wholecloth quilt has serious damage anywhere, except around the edges, there is not a lot that can be done, (other than recovering and requilting it, which would be a mammoth task requiring a professional). If it only has damage around the edges, it is retrievable. The impaired sides can be cut off and neatly hemmed. The geometry of the stitching designs will be slightly lost but the quilt will have a new lease of life. If the stitching patterns are exceptional and you just want to own the quilt to admire it, then leave it as it is, but don't expect to be able to use or wash it very often. People are inclined to throw up their hands in horror at the prospect of cutting a quilt down or using part of a badly damaged one for some other purpose. They are correct in doing so if the quilt is very early, very rare, or of historic interest, either because of who made it or the fabrics comprising it. I feel strongly that an historic quilt should be preserved as it is rather than being restored. I feel just as strongly that there is no harm in restoring or recycling a pretty everyday quilt, just as the original owners would have done. Is it better to have the quilt in circulation again, to be used and admired, even if it has lost a few inches, or, in more extreme cases, been made into cushions or other decorative objects.

Cushions. (Photograph: Hazel Newman).

Hearts. (Photograph: Hazel Newman).

When considering the price, take into account age, condition, rareness and quality of workmanship. Very few Welsh quilts in reasonable to good condition, bought today, will not appreciate in value. As a finite commodity that has increased in popularity, it cannot be otherwise, but always choose a quilt that will give you pleasure to own. Remember, Welsh quilting was a craft industry producing 'utilitarian' quilts made as bedding. Respect them, but do not revere them to the point where you cannot have them out where they can be seen and enjoyed.

Typical basket quilt akin to its American cousins.

Patchwork, Llandeilo, c.1830. The minute in the centre grow in size as they work their way towards the border giving a kaleidoscope effect.

A central star cotton patchwork made from a variety of floral and solid cottons, Brecon, c.1910.

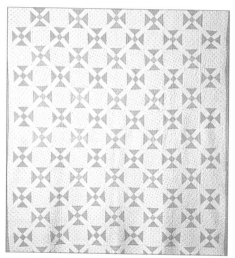

Neatly executed pink, blue and white Victorian patchwork, the Valleys.

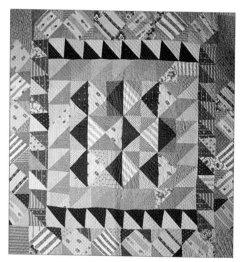

Dramatic mid 19th century, Pembrokeshire patchwork.

Satin cotton 'sample' quilt, Carmarthenshire, c.1920.

A good example of patchwork fabric, which is backed and quilted.
The effect is of patchwork, but it is printed rather than pieced.

Caring for Quilts

OST WELSH QUILTS WERE MADE FOR USE, and are appropriately hardy. The following are basic quidelines which I hope will be helpful to owners who want quilts that give them pleasure and are practical at the same time.

Although I listed a few 'don'ts' earlier in the book it is worth elaborating on them and offering a few positive suggestions regarding the general care and maintenance of quilts. We have discussed condition in terms of deterioration but another important factor is staining. Over the years I have come to recognise the stains that are easily removable and those that are permanent. It is always easier to tackle a stain if the quilt is washable. A quilt that can be laundered may be transformed by washing in a way that one that demands dry cleaning will not be. Most Welsh quilts were intended for the wash, but the flannels, and cottons using some of the early dyes, can be ruined if placed in soap and water. Early on, when quilts were only thought of as 'beddin'', this counted for little, and a housewife would place all her quilts on a slate slab to be doused with water, rubbed with a large cake of Sunlight, rubbed and scrubbed and then sluiced down with a fresh supply of rinse water. If the colours ran, the quilt still provided warmth, and when it was worn out it would be replaced. I have cried upon seeing most wonderful quilts that had been ruined by methods such as these. When buying a quilt, be sure to establish whether it is washable or not. A few general guidelines which may prove helpful are as follows:

1 Flannels and other woollen quilts should be dry-cleaned.
2 Strong colours, particularly reds, should be tested for colourfastness, which is easily done by placing the merest corner of the quilt in a tiny amount of lukewarm suds. If after a few minutes there is no sign of colour in the water (other than dirt!) it should be safe enough to wash the quilt. If there is evidence of running, dry-clean.

Washday by the stream.

3 Dry-clean a satin cotton quilt if it is in mint condition and has obviously never been washed before, as that way you will be able to maintain its sheen. (If a dingy fold mark, which has been caused by dust rather than by fading, exists then washing is preferable, as the fabric sheen will only dim slightly, whereas the marking is offensive).

4 Dry-clean a patchwork if it has never been washed before (you can tell this if the sizing is still evident in the fabrics).

5 A pastel patchwork is usually washable.

6 Red and white quilts are, for the most part, washable but always test first. It is advisable to wash all red and whites in cold water to which a good couple of tablespoons of salt have been added.

7 Cotton quilts, in excellent condition, lined with cotton, can be washed in a machine, but use a launderette or commercial one as it is too much of a strain on an ordinary domestic appliance. An all-cotton quilt can be machine dried as well, but take it out before it is bone-dry. While very slightly damp, place it on a sheet either on the lawn or on a bed while it finishes drying. That way you will not end up with creases.

8 Lambswool lined quilts that are washable must always be done by hand so as not to bunch the wool. They must be rinsed thoroughly, gently squeezed out and placed as flat as possible to dry. In the old days they would have been draped over the hedgerows. I have a series of parallel clotheslines which permit the air to circulate under as well as over the quilt. Avoid hanging the quilt vertically, as any residue not washed and rinsed out completely, will form little rust-like lines as it dries. If a lambswool filled quilt is washed in water that is too warm, or is placed in a hot drier, the wool will shrink, leaving the quilting hollow and shrivelled, and the wool will appear through the outer fabric. In some cases where shrinkage is slight, this wool can be shaved

Drying on the hedgerows.

Splendid silk patchwork from Llechryd, Cardiganshire, c.1830.
It features a fine combination of varying sizes of rectangles
and tumbling blocks.

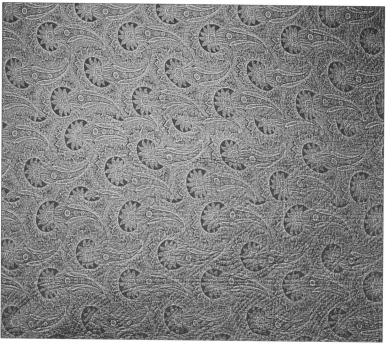

Typical red paisley Welsh quilt, c.1900. Good stitching
patterns are partially obscured by the dramatic fabric.

Printed panel red paisley.

A superb stack of early 'gritty' Welsh blankets.

with a safety razor. When this is done with great care, the quilt is not damaged and it is no longer unsightly.

9 Always use soap rather than detergent, as chemicals are not good for old fabrics. One of the best products I have found for washing quilts, believe it or not, is horse shampoo! It was recommended to me by an American quilter as safe and effective – and so it has proved.

10 Do use a gentle conditioner in the final rinse. This makes the quilt softer and less rigid.

11 If a washable quilt is very dingy or slightly marked, I soak it in a gentle pre-soak overnight before washing.

12 Stains must be dealt with extremely carefully. Commercial stain removers are occasionally used if the quilt is sturdy and is to be washed immediately afterwards but if used on anything other than whites they are likely to remove some, if not all, of the colour as well. A good tip for removing rust mould, which is commonly found on old fabrics, non-chemically, is to squeeze lemon juice onto the spot, then salt, then more lemon juice. Let it dry, remove the hardened salt, and then repeat the process. You may have to do this several times, but persevere, as you will succeed. Watermarks or any ringed stains can be dealt with, on a washable quilt, by rubbing glycerine into the ring, leaving it for several hours and then massaging washing-up liquid into the glycerine. Again leave it for a few hours prior to washing.

13 Old stains on a quilt to be dry-cleaned are very unlikely to come out, so weigh up in your mind whether or not you can live with the staining before purchasing. Old textiles must not be punished. It is better to accept a stain as part of the patina of age rather than destroy the fabric in an attempt to remove it.

14 Always choose a first class dry-cleaners with experience of old textiles.

15 If you own a quilt of great value it is essential that you have it speciality cleaned. This tends to be very expensive (between £30 and £200), but is well worth doing. One of the better museums, housing textiles, would probably advise you as to who to contact.

16 If you are hanging a quilt or using it on a bed, don't put it in direct sunlight, and, as I suggested earlier, don't store a quilt without keeping a sharp eye on it; refolding it frequently. Store it in a container that 'breathes', and don't forget adequate pest control.

Finally, don't be intimidated by all this advice. It is meant only to guide you. A quilt is a wonderful object and though old textiles are inclined to be fragile and must be looked after, a quilt is one of the most rewarding items you can bring into your home.

Conclusion

AS IS THE CASE WITH ANY CRAFT INDUSTRY, quiltmaking in Wales depended on those who devoted themselves to its success. The quilters created something that was in demand for a given period. A combination of a decrease in this demand, lack of adequate remuneration for the time involved, and the outbreak of World War Two, gradually ended this significant chapter in the history of Welsh craft industries. Only in retrospect can we recognise what an important role was played by the women who dedicated so much of their lives to the Welsh quilt. Without exaggerating, they can be, and should be, called the unsung artists of their day. As fewer and fewer quilts appear commercially, it is time for the finest of those that have come down to us to be exhibited more widely. It is time for them to be on view, as exemplary models for the quiltmakers of today. Now the best Welsh quilts must be recognised not only as the residue of a past craft industry but as essential components of the current art heritage of Wales.

Rachel and Emrys Jones hold up a satin cotton quilt outside their house in Llanybydder, Cardiganshire.
(Photograph: Janet Bridge).

Blankets

THERE ARE OVER ELEVEN MILLION sheep in Wales, according to the June 1996 Agricultural Census. In 1900 there were four million, and, at the middle of the last century, a mere two and a half million. Practically all Welsh textiles have been, and are, dependant on these animals. Paradoxically, as the flocks have multiplied the production of Welsh textiles has radically decreased. A century ago, the woollen industry in Wales was pivotal, with 300 mills operating in Carmarthenshire, Cardiganshire and Pembrokeshire alone. By 1947, only about 70 mills were recorded as remaining in the whole of Wales. This number has dwindled to the merest handful still existing at the present time. Although the woollen industry is now in the hands of a relatively tiny group of specialists, it, unlike the Welsh quilt, still survives as a craft industry. In this brief chapter, I shall concentrate on the blankets, coverlets and 'cartheni' made contemporaneously with quiltmaking's most prolific period, 1850–1940.

Although blankets and woollen cloth have always been woven in Wales, the reluctance of the small mill owners to embrace new technological innovations limited output and restricted design. From about 1825 onwards, the Welsh woollen industry was almost totally limited to supplying local communities, no longer attempting to cater to a wider clientele outside the country. This self-limitation, in a strange way, is what has given the 19th and early 20th century blankets their distinctive Welsh character. Due to environmental conditions and an irregular diet, sheep indigenous to Wales produced a comparatively rough fleece, and this is reflected in the graininess of many of the blankets (particularly the earlier ones). Once considered crude and unfashionable, the coarse 19th century blankets are the ones most sought after today. Interior decorators love what they refer to as the 'gritty' ones, and several of the top home furnishing designers have attempted to copy them.

Although plain, undyed, natural wool blankets were the most common, much of the fleece was dyed either before or after spinning, or as woven cloth. Synthetic dyes were introduced soon after 1855, but many of the smaller, more insular mills persisted in their use of natural dyes well into the 1930s. These include madder and cochineal for reds, woad and indigo for blues, and various berries and lichens for other shades and tints. Density of colour varied greatly, and repeats were unpredictable, but the subtlety of natural colours is what even today entices weavers to persevere in their use of them.

Although the numbers of Welsh blankets woven between 1850 to 1940 far exceeds the number of quilts surviving from the same period, they too were in danger of extinction. Lack of appreciation, bad washing and environmental hazards, particularly mice, moth and mould, resulted in the loss of vast numbers. It is only in the last decade or so that their unique qualities have been recognised and esteemed.

Types of Blankets

BLANKETS IN NATURAL CREAM were far more prevalent than those in other solid colours. The Welsh mill owners preferred to mix coloured yarns. Results varied greatly, depending on the knowledge, skill and taste of the weaver. Some were enormously subtle, whereas others were garish and offensive (comparable to the brash satin-cotton quilts mentioned previously!)

The earlier more primitive blankets are my favourites. Bold, vertical stripes in black, navy or brown were emblazoned on a natural cream background. Their appeal is similar to that of the stark geometric patchworks which they compliment so superbly. Nearly all the blankets in this category were made on a single loom and consist of two widths joined down the centre by hand. This was done either at the mill or by the purchaser at home. Before the turn of the century, single loom blankets were the norm. With the introduction of the double loom, many 20th century blankets were of one piece. Numerous smaller mills and individual weavers, however, never changed over to the wider loom thus producing narrow loom blankets in the twenties and thirties and even later.

'Gritty' 19th Century Welsh blankets.

John Evans, born in 1860, weaver by trade. To supplement his income he qualified for the position of Postmaster of Talgarreg, Cardiganshire, the prerequisites being that he was teetotal, a church goer, and a member of the Conservative party. Installing his loom in the back he continued his dual career for many years. By the time of his death in 1956 he was virtually blind.
(Photograph courtesy of Miss Rees of Talgarreg).

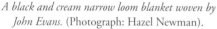

A black and cream narrow loom blanket woven by John Evans. (Photograph: Hazel Newman).

Plaids, woven before the turn of the century on narrow looms, were almost invariably strong, dark colours against a natural cream field. Later plaids were inclined to utilise more colours within each blanket, and there was a predilection for pastels.

Many Welsh blankets are fringed top and bottom, but a true carthen or 'fringed quilt' was to be used as a bedspread as well as a blanket, and was surrounded by fringing on all four sides.

Another dual purpose blanket/coverlet was the honeycomb quilt which resembles a waffle and was designed to enmesh pockets of air, thus producing a thermal effect.

20th century fringed, plaid blankets woven in the 1920's. (Photograph: Hazel Newman).

Probably considered the most typically Welsh of all woollen covers was the 'tapestry' quilt. This was not made from tapestry at all but rather a double-ply woollen yarn, and it is now in every tourist shop in Wales in the guise of spectacle cases, ladies capes, pocketbooks and tea cosies. Originally, this double-cloth was woven for practical, hardwearing bedcovers. Some of the early patterns appeared concurrently in double-weave wool covers produced in Germany, the United States and Wales. At the American museum in Bath there is a strippy all-wool double-weave narrow loom coverlet with a 'snowball' design dated 1840. I have seen its double on my travels here in Wales. Doubtless, interaction between immigrant weavers both here and abroad is responsible for this phenomenon. Some of the older tapestries were very beautiful. The colours were more subtle, the weave closer, and the designs more intricate and varied than in the two or three patterns available today.

Happily, some fine imaginative Welsh blankets are once again being designed and woven but, unfortunately, mainly for a foreign market. Is it possible that, struck by the warmth and beauty of such worthy antecedents, the Welsh will soon be using them to replace their duvets? It is my fervent hope, now there is an awareness and appreciation of the true quality of the Welsh blanket, those existing will be preserved and elevated to their rightful position within the hierarchy of Welsh crafts. It would be wonderful if more of the defunct mills were restored, permitting a uniquely Welsh commodity to be produced in greater numbers once again.

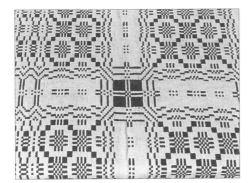 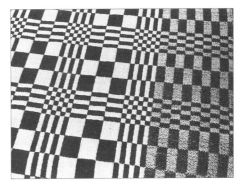

Three examples of 19th century tapestry bedcovers.

Public Collections of Quilts and Blankets

The Welsh Folk Museum, St Fagans (Quilts & Blankets)
The Welsh Woollen Museum, Drefach Felindre (primarily blankets)
The American Museum Bath, (for comparisons between American and Welsh quilts and woven coverlet designs)
Llanidloes, (Projected Quilt Exhibition Centre)

Bibliography

M. FitzRandolph: *Traditional Quilting*, Batsford.
Ilid E. Anthony: *Quilting & Patchwork in Wales*, Amgueddfa.
Janet Rae: *Quilts of the British Isles*, Constable.
Dorothy Osler: *Traditional British Quilts*, Batsford.
Barbara Chaney: *The Essential Quilter*, David & Charles
Michele Walker: *The Passionate Quilter*, Ebury Press.
Christine Stevens: *Quilts*, Gomer Press.
Quilters Guild: *Quilt Treasures*, Deidre MacDonald Books.
Sheila Betterton: *More Quilts & Coverlets*, American Museum in Britain.
Ann Sutton: *The Textiles of Wales*, Bellew.

*Mrs Nance Davis of Cwmsychpant, Cardiganshire, and her sister, Vi, proudly display
blankets woven from the wool of their own sheep.*
(Photograph: Hazel Newman).